The Diamond Sutra: The Perfection of Wisdom

TRANSLATED TO CHINESE BY TRIPIṬAKA
MASTER KUMARAJIVA, JIN DYNASTY (YAO QIN)
TRANSLATED TO ENGLISH BY JULIE ZHU

Bamboo & Pine Press

©2025 Julie Zhu
Published by: Bamboo & Pine Press (Zhu & Song Press, LLC)
North Potomac, Maryland 20878

Editor-in-Chief: Xiaohong Zhu
Editorial Contact:
editor@zhuandsongpress.com
Cover Design: Zhu & Song Media
Publisher Website:
www.zhuandsongpress.com
Printed in: USA, UK
Distribution: Worldwide

ISBN-13: 978-1-950797-78-3
eBook ISBN-13: 978-1-950797-79-0

All rights reserved.

Preface to the Publication

The Buddhist scriptures are as vast as the great ocean and as brilliant as a sky full of stars. Yet for modern readers, it can feel difficult to know where to begin — and few have the time to study them all.

In truth, among the many Buddhist texts, there are two that stand above the rest, each word precious and profound. Reading these two is equivalent to absorbing the very essence of Buddhism. Moreover, both are concise and refined — perfectly suited for modern people to read, recite, and reflect upon in daily life to cultivate inner peace and virtue.

These two scriptures are THE DIAMOND SUTRA and THE HEART SUTRA. Of these, THE HEART SUTRA is particularly short — just two pages long — and thus cannot form a standalone book. Therefore, Bamboo & Pine Press has included it as an appendix, for readers' convenience and easy reference.

THE DIAMOND SUTRA is also relatively short. Bamboo & Pine Press has previously published it as part of THE TEN GREAT BUDDHIST SUTRAS, but it is somewhat inconvenient to flip through such a thick volume daily just to read THE DIAMOND SUTRA. Hence, this time, Bamboo & Pine Press is publishing it separately, making it easier for Buddhist practitioners and enthusiasts to carry, read, and recite at any time.

If this publication brings even a little convenience or benefit to students of Buddhism, then our purpose has been fulfilled.

May your reading bring you joy and fill you with the bliss of Dharma.

Xiaohong Zhu
President, Bamboo & Pine Press

03/26/2022

Supplementary Note on the English Edition:

After the Simplified Chinese edition of the DIAMOND SUTRA was published in 2022, it was very well received by the public. Therefore, we have now made the heartfelt decision to publish an English edition, and we hope everyone will enjoy it.

Xiaohong Zhu
President, Bamboo & Pine Press

10/22/2025

Table of Contents

The Diamond Sutra: The Perfection of Wisdom 9

Appendix: The Heart of the Perfection of Wisdom Sutra 67

The Diamond Sutra: The Perfection of Wisdom

TRANSLATED BY TRIPIṬAKA MASTER KUMARAJIVA, JIN DYNASTY (YAO QIN)
TRANSLATED TO ENGLISH BY JULIE ZHU

Thus have I heard:

At one time, the Buddha was staying in the Kingdom of Shravasti, in the Jeta Grove of Anathapindada's Park, together with a great assembly of 1,250 monks.

At that time, when it was mealtime, the World-Honored One put on his robe, took his alms bowl, and entered the great city of Shravasti to beg for food. Within the city, he went from house to house in order. After completing his alms round, he returned to his dwelling place. When he had finished his meal, he put away his robe and bowl, washed his feet, arranged his seat, and sat down.

Then the Venerable Subhuti, who was among the assembly, rose from his seat, uncovered his right shoulder, knelt with his right knee on the ground, joined his palms respectfully, and said to the Buddha:

"Rare indeed, World-Honored One! The Tathagata skillfully protects and cares for all bodhisattvas, and skillfully entrusts them with guidance. World-Honored One, for good men and good women who have aroused the mind of Anuttara-samyak-sambodhi (the unsurpassed, perfect enlightenment), how should they abide their mind? How should they subdue their thoughts?"

The Buddha said:
"Excellent, excellent, Subhuti! Just as you have spoken, the Tathagata skillfully protects and cares for all bodhisattvas, and skillfully entrusts them with guidance. Now listen attentively, and I shall tell you: for good men and good women who have aroused the mind of Anuttara-samyak-sambodhi, they should abide and subdue their minds in this way."

Subhuti said: "Yes indeed, World-Honored One! We are delighted and wish to hear."

The Buddha said to Subhuti:

"All great bodhisattvas should thus subdue their minds. Of all the kinds of living beings — whether born from eggs, from wombs, from moisture, or by transformation; whether they have form or are formless; whether they have perception, lack perception, or are neither with nor without perception —I will liberate them by leading them to Nirvana without residue.

Although countless, immeasurable, and boundless beings have thus been liberated, in truth, not a single being has been liberated.

Why is this so, Subhuti? If a bodhisattva holds the notions of a self, a person, a sentient being, or a life span, then he is not truly a bodhisattva.

Furthermore, Subhuti, a bodhisattva should practice giving (dana) without attachment. That is, he should not give while abiding in forms, nor in sounds, scents, tastes, tactile objects, or dharmas.

Subhuti, a bodhisattva should give in this manner — without attachment to appearances. Why? Because if a bodhisattva gives without attachment to appearances, his merit and virtue are beyond measure.

Subhuti, what do you think? Is the space in the east measurable?"

"No, World-Honored One."

"Subhuti, is the space in the south, west, north, in the four directions, above and below, measurable?"

"No, World-Honored One."

"In the same way, Subhuti, the merit of a bodhisattva who gives without attachment to appearances is likewise beyond measure.

Subhuti, a bodhisattva should abide as I have taught.

Subhuti, what do you think? Can the Tathagata be seen through physical form?"

"No, World-Honored One. The Tathagata cannot be seen through physical form. Why? Because what the Tathagata calls 'form' is not truly form."

The Buddha said to Subhuti:
"All forms are illusory. If one perceives that all forms are not truly forms, then one sees the Tathagata."

Subhuti said to the Buddha:
"World-Honored One, will there be any beings who, hearing such words and phrases, are able to give rise to true faith?"

The Buddha replied:
"Do not say that, Subhuti. After the Tathagata's passing, in the last five hundred years, there will be those who keep the precepts and cultivate good deeds. Hearing these words and phrases, they will give rise to faith and take them as true. You should know, Subhuti, that such people are not those who have planted good roots under just one Buddha, or two, or three, or even four or five Buddhas, but have already planted good roots under countless millions of Buddhas. When they hear these words and give rise to pure faith,

even for a single moment, the Tathagata fully knows and fully sees them, and they will obtain immeasurable merit and virtue.

Why is this so? Because such beings no longer hold to the notions of a self, a person, a sentient being, or a life span.

They also do not hold to the notion of a "dharma," nor to the notion of "no dharma." Why is this so? If their minds grasp at appearances, they become attached to the idea of self, person, sentient being, and life span.

If they grasp at the appearance of dharmas, that is attachment to self, person, sentient being, and life span. If they grasp at the appearance of "no dharmas," that too is attachment to self, person, sentient being, and life span. Therefore, one should neither grasp at dharmas nor at "no dharmas."

For this reason, the Tathagata often says: 'Monks, you should know that the Dharma I teach is like a raft — once you have crossed the river, you should abandon it. How much more so should you abandon that which is not the Dharma.'

Subhuti, what do you think? Has the Tathagata attained unsurpassed, perfect enlightenment (Anuttara-samyak-sambodhi)? Has the Tathagata spoken any Dharma?"

Subhuti replied:
"World-Honored One, as I understand the meaning of what the Buddha has said, there is no fixed Dharma called unsurpassed, perfect enlightenment, nor is

there any definite Dharma that the Tathagata can speak. Why is this so? Because the Dharma that the Tathagata speaks cannot be grasped, cannot be expressed in words; it is neither Dharma nor non-Dharma.

Why is this so? Because all sages and noble ones are distinguished from others through the realization of the unconditioned Dharma."

The Buddha said:
"Subhuti, what do you think? If someone were to fill a trichiliocosm with the seven precious treasures and give them in charity, would the merit of that person be great?"

Subhuti replied:
"Very great indeed, World-Honored One. Why is this so? Because that merit is not

of the nature of merit — and for this reason, the Tathagata says that the merit is great."

The Buddha said:
"If there is someone who receives, upholds, and expounds even four lines of verse from this sutra to others, the merit of that person will surpass that of the one who gives away the seven precious treasures filling a trichiliocosm.

Why is this so, Subhuti? Because all Buddhas, and the Dharma of unsurpassed, perfect enlightenment (Anuttara-samyak-sambodhi) realized by all Buddhas, arise from this very sutra.

Subhuti, what is called the 'Buddha' and the 'Dharma' is, in truth, not Buddha and not Dharma."

The Buddha asked:

"What do you think, Subhuti? Can a Srotapanna (stream-enterer) think to himself, 'I have attained the fruit of stream-entry'?"

Subhuti replied:

"No, World-Honored One. Why not? The term Srotapanna means 'one who has entered the stream,' yet in reality, there is no entry — not into forms, sounds, scents, tastes, tangible objects, or mental phenomena. Therefore, he is called a stream-enterer."

The Buddha asked:

"What do you think, Subhuti? Can a Sakridagamin (once-returner) think, 'I have attained the fruit of once-returning'?"

Subhuti replied:

"No, World-Honored One. Why not? The term Sakridagamin means 'one who returns once,' yet in reality there is neither coming nor going. Therefore, he is called a once-returner."

The Buddha asked:
"What do you think, Subhuti? Can an anagamin (non-returner) think, 'I have attained the fruit of non-returning'?"

Subhuti replied:
"No, World-Honored One. Why not? The term anagamin means 'one who does not return,' yet in truth there is no such thing as not returning. Therefore, he is called a non-returner."

The Buddha asked:
"What do you think, Subhuti? Can an arhat think, 'I have attained the path of

arhatship'?"

Subhuti replied:
"No, World-Honored One. Why not? In reality, there is no such Dharma as arhatship.

World-Honored One, if an arhat were to think, 'I have attained arhatship,' then he would be attached to the notions of self, person, sentient being, and life span.

World-Honored One, the Buddha has said that I, Subhuti, have attained the Samadhi of Peaceful Liberation and am foremost among those free from desire, the foremost arhat. Yet, World-Honored One, I do not think to myself, 'I am a desireless arhat.'

World-Honored One, if I thought, 'I have

attained the path of arhatship,' then you would not say that Subhuti delights in the practice of quiet retreat.

Why is this so? Because in truth, Subhuti has no practice to engage in — and that is why he is called one who delights in the practice of quiet retreat."

The Buddha said to Subhuti:
"What do you think? When the Tathagata was with DipamkaraBuddha (the Buddha of the Burning Lamp), did he attain any Dharma?"

Subhuti replied:
"No, World-Honored One. When the Tathagata was with Dipamkara Buddha, he in truth attained no Dharma."

The Buddha said:

"What do you think, Subhuti? Do bodhisattvas adorn the Buddha lands?"

Subhuti replied:
"No, World-Honored One. Why not? Because what is called 'adornment of the Buddha land' is, in truth, no adornment — and that is why it is called adornment."

The Buddha continued:
"Therefore, Subhuti, great bodhisattvas should give rise to a pure mind — a mind that does not abide in form, sound, scent, taste, touch, or dharma.
They should generate the mind that does not abide anywhere."

The Buddha asked:
"Subhuti, suppose someone had a body as great as Mount Sumeru, the king of mountains — what do you think? Would

that be a great body?"

Subhuti replied:
"Very great indeed, World-Honored One. But the Buddha says that what is called a 'body' is not truly a body — therefore it is called a great body."

The Buddha said:
"Subhuti, if the number of grains of sand in the River Ganges were used to count as many Ganges Rivers, what do you think? Would the sands of all those Ganges Rivers be many?"

Subhuti said:
"Very many, World-Honored One! Even the Ganges Rivers themselves are innumerable—how much more so the sands within them!"

The Buddha said:

"Subhuti, I now tell you the truth: if a good man or good woman were to fill as many trichiliocosms as there are grains of sand in those Ganges Rivers with the seven precious treasures, and give them all away in charity, would that person gain great merit?"

Subhuti replied:

"Very great indeed, World-Honored One!"

The Buddha said:

"Yet, Subhuti, if a good man or good woman were to receive, uphold, and teach even four lines of verse from this sutra to others, the merit of that person would far surpass the previous one.

Furthermore, Subhuti, wherever this sutra is spoken, even if only four lines of verse are recited, you should know that this place is to be venerated by all beings of the world — gods, humans, and asuras alike — as if it were a stupa or temple of the Buddha. How much more so should one honor those who are able to fully receive, recite, and uphold it!

Subhuti, you should know that such a person accomplishes the supreme, most rare, and most excellent Dharma. Wherever this sutra is found, that place should be regarded as one where the Buddha is present, honored by his disciples."

At that time, Subhuti said to the Buddha: "World-Honored One, what should this sutra be called, and how should we uphold it?"

The Buddha replied:

"This sutra shall be called The Diamond prajna paramita Sutra (The Diamond Sutra of Transcendent Wisdom). By this name you should uphold it.

Why is that? Subhuti, the Buddha has said that 'prajna paramita' is not truly prajna paramita — it is merely called prajna paramita.

Subhuti, what do you think? Has the Tathagata spoken any Dharma?"

Subhuti said:
"World-Honored One, the Tathagata has spoken nothing."

The Buddha said:
"Subhuti, what do you think? Are the fine particles that make up the trichiliocosms

many?"

Subhuti said:
"Very many, World-Honored One."

The Buddha said:
"Subhuti, those fine particles are not truly fine particles; they are merely called fine particles. Likewise, when the Tathagata speaks of a 'world,' it is not truly a world — it is merely called a world."

The Buddha said:
"Subhuti, what do you think? Can the Tathagata be recognized by means of his thirty-two physical attributes?"

Subhuti said:
"No, World-Honored One. The Tathagata cannot be recognized by means of his thirty-two physical attributes. Why?

Because what the Tathagata calls the thirty-two physical attributes are not truly attributes — therefore they are called the thirty-two physical attributes."

The Buddha said:
"If a good man or good woman were to give up as many lives as there are grains of sand in the Ganges Rivers for charity, and another person were to receive, uphold, and expound even four lines of this sutra to others, the latter would gain far greater merit."

Upon hearing this sermon, Subhuti was moved to tears, having deeply understood its meaning and significance. He said to the Buddha:

"Rare indeed, World-Honored One! The Buddha has spoken such a profound and wondrous scripture. From the time I first obtained the wisdom eye until now, I have never before heard such a sutra.

World-Honored One, if there are people who hear this sutra and give rise to pure faith, they will realize the truth of ultimate reality. You should know that such a person has achieved the foremost and most rare merit.

World-Honored One, what is called 'ultimate reality' (suchness) is, in truth, not a reality; therefore the Tathagata calls it ultimate reality.

World-Honored One, it is not difficult for me to hear, believe, understand, and uphold this sutra. But in the future, five hundred years after your passing, if there are beings who can hear this sutra, believe, understand, and uphold it, such people will truly be most rare.

Why? Because such persons will have no attachment to the notions of self, person, sentient being, or life span.

Why is this so? Because what is called the notion of self is not truly self; and the notions of person, sentient being, and life span are not truly such notions either.

Why? Because one who is free from all notions and appearances is called a Buddha."

The Buddha said to Subhuti:
"Yes, indeed, Subhuti, it is just as you say! If there are people who, upon hearing this sutra, are neither startled, frightened, nor afraid, you should know that such a person

is exceedingly rare.

Why is this so? Subhuti, what the Tathagata calls the first perfection (paramita) is not truly the first perfection; therefore it is called the first perfection.

Subhuti, what the Tathagata calls the Perfection of Patience (KSANTI paramita) is not truly patience; therefore it is called patience.

Why is this so? Subhuti, in the past, when I was the Sage of Patience and my body was cut to pieces by King Kali, even then I had no perception of self, no perception of others, no perception of sentient beings, and no perception of life span.

Why? Subhuti, if at that time I had had a perception of self, of others, of sentient beings, or of life span, I would have given rise to anger and resentment.

Subhuti, I also recall that for five hundred lifetimes in the past I was the Sage who practiced patience. During all those lifetimes, I had no perception of self, of others, of sentient beings, or of life span.

Therefore, Subhuti, a Bodhisattva should abandon all appearances and give rise to the mind of ANUTTARA SAMYAKSAMBODHI (Unsupassed Perfect Enlightenment).
He should not give rise to a mind attached to form;
he should not give rise to a mind attached to sound, smell, taste, touch, or dharmas. He should give rise to a mind that is not attached anywhere.

If the mind is attached, it is not truly a mind of non-attachment.

Therefore, the Buddha says:
A Bodhisattva should give alms without being attached to form.

Subhuti, a Bodhisattva gives alms for the benefit of all beings, yet he should give in this way — without attachment.

The Tathagata says that all appearances are not appearances, and this is why they are called appearances.
He also says: all sentient beings are not truly sentient beings — and this is why they are called sentient beings.

Subhuti, the Tathagata is one who speaks truthfully, who speaks what is real, who speaks what accords with reality, who does not speak deceitfully, and who does not speak differently from truth.

Subhuti, the Dharma the Tathagata has obtained is neither real nor unreal.

Subhuti, if a Bodhisattva's mind abides in dharmas while practicing generosity, it is like entering darkness — he sees nothing. But if his mind does not abide in dharmas while practicing generosity, it is like having eyes in bright sunlight — he can see all kinds of forms clearly.

Subhuti, in the future, if there are good men or good women who can receive, uphold, read, and recite this sutra, the Tathagata will know and see them all with his Buddha wisdom, and they will all accomplish immeasurable and boundless merit.

Subhuti, if a good man or good woman renounces their life for charity in the morning as many times as there are grains of sand in the Ganges, and does likewise at noon and in the evening, continuing thus for immeasurable hundreds of thousands of millions of kalpas — and if another person, upon hearing this sutra, gives rise to pure faith without opposition — the merit of the latter exceeds that of the former.

How much more so if one writes, upholds, reads, recites, and expounds it for others!

In summary, Subhuti, this sutra possesses inconceivable, immeasurable, and boundless merit.

The Tathagata speaks it for those who have embarked upon the Great Vehicle, for those who aspire to the Supreme Vehicle.

If there are people who can receive, uphold, read, recite, and extensively explain it for others, the Tathagata knows and sees them — all such people will accomplish immeasurable, incalculable, boundless, and inconceivable merit.

Such people are truly carrying the Tathagata's ANUTTARA SAMYAKSAMBODHI on their shoulders.

Why is this so, Subhuti?
Because those who delight in lesser teachings, who cling to the view of self, the view of others, the view of sentient beings, or the view of life span — such people are unable to hear, receive, read, or recite this sutra, nor can they explain it to

others."

The Buddha said to Subhuti:

"Subhuti, wherever this sutra is found — in any place whatsoever — all beings of the world, including devas (heavenly beings), humans, and asuras (demigods), should offer reverence to it. You should know that this place is like a stupa (a sacred shrine). All should honor it, make obeisance, and circumambulate it, scattering flowers and incense around it in worship.

Furthermore, Subhuti, if good men and good women receive, uphold, read, and recite this sutra, and they are looked down upon or despised by others, it is because in past lives they created negative karma that would have caused them to fall into the evil paths of existence.

Now, because they are treated with contempt by people in this life, their past karma is thereby eliminated, and they will attain ANUTTARA SAMYAKSAMBODHI (Unsupassed Perfect Enlightenment).

Subhuti, I recall that in the distant past, through countless asamkhyeya kalpas (immeasurable eons), before the Buddha Dipankara (the Buddha of the Lamp of Wisdom), I encountered and served eighty-four hundred thousand million nayutas of Buddhas. I honored and attended upon all of them without ever failing to do so.

Yet, if there were a person in the future Dharma-ending age who could receive, uphold, read, and recite this sutra, the merit they would obtain would surpass mine by far. Indeed, even the merit I gained from honoring and serving all those Buddhas would not compare to a hundredth part, or even a thousandth, ten thousandth, hundred millionth part — in fact, no comparison, calculation, or analogy could reach it.

Subhuti, if I were to explain in full the merits of those good men and good women who will, in the Dharma-ending age, receive, uphold, read, and recite this sutra, there might be those who, upon hearing it, would become suspicious, skeptical, even bewildered.

Therefore, Subhuti, you should know that the meaning of this sutra is inconceivable, and its fruits and rewards are likewise inconceivable.

At that time, Subhuti asked the Buddha:
"World-Honored One, if good men and good women wish to give rise to the mind of ANUTTARA SAMYAKSAMBODHI, how should they abide their minds, and how should they subdue them?"

The Buddha replied:
"Good men and good women who wish to give rise to the mind of ANUTTARA SAMYAKSAMBODHI should thus give rise to this thought:
'I must lead all sentient beings to final Nirvana — to liberate them all from suffering. Yet, after liberating countless beings, I realize that not a single being has truly been liberated.'

Why is this so, Subhuti? Because if a Bodhisattva clings to the notion of a self, a person, a being, or a life span, then he is not a true Bodhisattva.

Why? Subhuti, there truly is no Dharma by which one can give rise to ANUTTARA SAMYAKSAMBODHI.

Subhuti, what do you think? Did the Tathagata obtain ANUTTARA SAMYAKSAMBODHI from the Buddha Dipankara?"

Subhuti replied:
"No, World-Honored One. As I understand the meaning of the Buddha's teaching, when the Buddha was before Dipankara Buddha, there was no Dharma by which he attained ANUTTARA SAMYAKSAMBODHI."

The Buddha said:
"Exactly so, exactly so, Subhuti. In truth, there is no Dharma through which the Tathagata attains ANUTTARA SAMYAKSAMBODHI.

If there had been such a Dharma, Dipankara Buddha would not have prophesied to me, saying:
'In the future, you will become a Buddha named Sakyamuni.'

Because there is truly no Dharma by which one attains ANUTTARA SAMYAKSAMBODHI, therefore Dipankara Buddha made that prophecy, saying:
'In the future, you will become a Buddha named Sakyamuni.'

Why is this so? Because "Tathagata"

means one who accords with Suchness (the true nature of all dharmas).

If someone were to say that the Tathagata attained ANUTTARA SAMYAKSAMBODHI, Subhuti, that would not be correct — for there is truly no Dharma by which the Buddha attains ANUTTARA SAMYAKSAMBODHI.

Subhuti, the ANUTTARA SAMYAKSAMBODHI attained by the Tathagata is neither real nor unreal. Therefore the Tathagata says that all dharmas are Buddha dharmas.

Subhuti, what the Tathagata calls 'all dharmas' are in fact not all dharmas; therefore they are called 'all dharmas.'

Subhuti, take the example of a person with

an immense, perfect body."

Subhuti said:
"World-Honored One, as the Tathagata has said: the person with the immense, perfect body has no such body; therefore it is called an immense, perfect body."

The Buddha said:
"Subhuti, it is the same with a Bodhisattva. If a Bodhisattva should think, 'I will liberate countless sentient beings,' he should not be called a Bodhisattva.

Why is this so?
Because, Subhuti, in reality there is no such dharma that can be called a Bodhisattva.
Therefore the Buddha says: 'All dharmas are without self, without person, without being, and without life span.'

Subhuti, if a Bodhisattva should think, 'I will adorn the Buddha land,' he should not be called a Bodhisattva.

Why is this so?

Because the Tathagata says, 'Adorning the Buddha land is not truly adorning; therefore it is called adorning.'

Subhuti, a Bodhisattva who thoroughly understands the principle of non-self in both persons and dharmas — the Tathagata calls that one a true Bodhisattva."

The Buddha continued:

"Subhuti, what do you think?
Does the Tathagata have the physical eye?"

Subhuti replied:

"Yes, World-Honored One, the Tathagata has the physical eye."

"Subhuti, what do you think?
Does the Tathagata have the divine eye?"

"Yes, World-Honored One, the Tathagata has the divine eye."

"Subhuti, what do you think?
Does the Tathagata have the wisdom eye?"

"Yes, World-Honored One, the Tathagata has the wisdom eye."

"Subhuti, what do you think?
Does the Tathagata have the Dharma eye?"

"Yes, World-Honored One, the Tathagata has the Dharma eye."

"Subhuti, what do you think?
Does the Tathagata have the Buddha eye?"

"Yes, World-Honored One, the Tathagata has the Buddha eye."

The Buddha said:
"Subhuti, what do you think? The sands in the Ganges River — did the Tathagata say they are sand?"

Subhuti replied:
"Yes, World-Honored One, the Tathagata said they are sand."

The Buddha said:
"Subhuti, if there were as many Ganges Rivers as there are grains of sand in the Ganges, and within each of those Ganges Rivers there were again as many grains of sand as there are in the Ganges itself —

would the number of those grains of sand be many?"

Subhuti said:
"Very many, World-Honored One!"

The Buddha said:
"Subhuti, in all those countless worlds as numerous as those grains of sand, the Tathagata fully knows the different thoughts of all sentient beings dwelling in them.

Why is this so?
Because the Tathagata says: 'All minds are not truly minds; therefore they are called minds.'

Why is this so?
Because the past mind cannot be obtained, the present mind cannot be obtained, and

the future mind cannot be obtained."

The Buddha continued:

"Subhuti, what do you think?
If someone were to fill the trichiliocosm world systems with the seven treasures and use them all in giving alms, wouldn't this person's merit be great?"

Subhuti said:
"Yes, World-Honored One, this person's merit from such an act would be extremely great."

The Buddha said:
"Subhuti, if merit had a real nature, the Tathagata would not have said that the merit is great.
It is precisely because merit has no self-nature that the Tathagata says that the

merit is great."

"Subhuti, what do you think?
Can the Tathagata be seen by means of his perfect form and body?"

Subhuti said:
"No, World-Honored One. The Tathagata cannot be seen by means of his perfect physical form.

Why is this so?
Because the Tathagata has said that 'perfect physical form' is not truly a perfect form; therefore it is called a perfect form."

"Subhuti, what do you think?
Can the Tathagata be seen by means of his perfect attributes?"

Subhuti said:

"No, World-Honored One. The Tathagata cannot be seen by means of his perfect attributes.

Why is this so?
Because the Tathagata has said: 'perfect attributes' are actually not perfect attributes. Therefore they are called perfect attributes.'"

"Subhuti, do not think that the Tathagata has the thought, 'I will teach a Dharma.' You must not think in this way.

Why is this so?
If anyone says that the Tathagata teaches a Dharma, they slander the Buddha, for they do not understand the meaning of what I teach.

Subhuti, when one speaks of 'teaching the

Dharma,' in reality there is no Dharma that can be spoken.
That is why it is called 'teaching the Dharma.'"

At that time, the wise Subhuti said to the Buddha:
"World-Honored One, in the future, will there be beings who hear this Dharma and give rise to faith?"

The Buddha replied:
"Subhuti, they are not truly beings, nor are they not beings.

Why is this so?
Subhuti, the 'beings' that people speak of — the Tathagata says they are not truly beings; therefore they are called beings."

Subhuti asked the Buddha:

"World-Honored One, the Buddha attained ANUTTARA SAMYAKSAMBODHI — did he actually attain nothing?"

The Buddha said:
"Exactly so, Subhuti. As to ANUTTARA SAMYAKSAMBODHI, I have not attained the slightest thing; that is why it is called ANUTTARA SAMYAKSAMBODHI."

"Furthermore, Subhuti, all Dharmas are perfectly equal — there is no high or low; this too is called ANUTTARA SAMYAKSAMBODHI.

By practicing all wholesome dharmas without self, without person, without being, and without life span, one attains ANUTTARA SAMYAKSAMBODHI.

Subhuti, what the Tathagata calls wholesome dharmas are in fact not truly wholesome dharmas; therefore they are called wholesome dharmas."

"Subhuti, if someone were to give away all the treasures of Mount Sumeru across the trichiliocosm, and another person were to receive, uphold, read, recite, and explain even four lines from this PRAJNAPARAMITA SUTRA to others, the merit of the latter would far exceed that of the former.

Even a hundredth, a thousandth, a millionth part of the former merit would not compare; in fact, no calculation or analogy could reach it."

"Subhuti, what do you think? Do not think that the Tathagata has the

thought, 'I must liberate beings.'
Subhuti, you must not think this way.

Why is this so?
Because in truth there are no beings that the Tathagata liberates.
If there were beings that the Tathagata liberated, then there would be a self, a person, a being, or a life span.

Subhuti, the Tathagata says: if there is a self, it is not truly a self; yet ordinary people take it as a self.
Subhuti, the Tathagata says: ordinary people are not truly ordinary people; therefore they are called ordinary people."

"Subhuti, what do you think?
Can the Tathagata be seen through the thirty-two physical attributes?"

Subhuti said:
"Yes, World-Honored One, the Tathagata can be seen through the thirty-two physical attributes"

The Buddha said:
"Subhuti, if one sees the Tathagata through the thirty-two physical attributes, then even a wheel-turning sage king would be called a Tathagata."

Subhuti said to the Buddha:
"World-Honored One, as I understand the meaning of your teaching, one should not view the Tathagata through the thirty-two physical attributes."

Then the World-Honored One spoke this verse:

"If one sees me in forms

> And seeks me in sounds,
> That person walks a wrong path
> And cannot see the Tathagata."

"Subhuti, if you think, 'The Tathagata attained ANUTTARA SAMYAKSAMBODHI not by virtue of his perfect attributes,' you should not think this way.

Subhuti, if you think, 'The Tathagata attained ANUTTARA SAMYAKSAMBODHI not because of his perfect attributes,' you should not think this way.

Subhuti, if one thinks in this way, that by giving rise to the mind of ANUTTARA SAMYAKSAMBODHI, all dharmas are extinguished, you should not think so.

Why is this so?

Because one who gives rise to the mind of ANUTTARA SAMYAKSAMBODHI does not say that dharmas are truly extinguished."

"Subhuti, if a Bodhisattva were to give away all the treasures of countless worlds, and if another person understands that all dharmas are without self and attains perfection in patience (KSANTI), the latter Bodhisattva surpasses the former in merit.

Why is this so, Subhuti?
Because the Bodhisattvas of such understanding do not seek or receive merit as a possession."

Subhuti said to the Buddha:
"World-Honored One, how is it that a Bodhisattva does not receive merit?"

The Buddha said:
"Subhuti, the merit that a Bodhisattva creates should not be clung to or grasped; therefore it is said that the Bodhisattva does not receive merit."

"Subhuti, if someone says: 'The Tathagata comes or goes, sits or lies down,' that person does not understand the meaning of what I teach.

Why is this so?
The Tathagata has no place from which he comes and no place to which he goes; therefore he is called the Tathagata."

"Subhuti, if a good man or good woman were to break the trichiliocosm into dust, what do you think — would the number of dust particles be great?"

Subhuti replied:

"Very great, World-Honored One. If those dust particles truly existed, the Buddha would not call them dust particles.

Why is this so? The Buddha says: the dust particles are not truly dust particles; therefore they are called dust particles.

World-Honored One, the trichiliocosm world systems spoken of by the Tathagata are not truly worlds; therefore they are called worlds.

Why is this so?
If a world truly existed, it would be one whole form. The Tathagata says: one whole form is not truly one whole form; therefore it is called one whole form."

The Buddha said:

"Subhuti, the 'one whole form' cannot truly be spoken of; yet ordinary people cling to it with desire.

Subhuti, if someone says: 'The Buddha spoke of my-view, person-view, being-view, life-view,' what do you think? Does that person understand the meaning of what I teach?"

Subhuti said:
"No, World-Honored One. That person does not understand the meaning of the Tathagata's teaching.

Why is this so?
World-Honored One says: my-view, person-view, being-view, and life-view are not truly my-view, person-view, being-view, or life-view; therefore they are called my-view, person-view, being-view,

and life-view."

"Subhuti, one who gives rise to the mind of ANUTTARA SAMYAKSAMBODHI should understand all dharmas in this way, see them in this way, and have faith and comprehension in this way — without ever giving rise to the view of a dharma-form (DHARMALAKSANA).

Subhuti, what is called a dharma-form is in fact not a dharma-form; therefore it is called a dharma-form."

"Subhuti, if someone were to give away all the treasures of an infinite number of countless worlds, yet a good man or good woman who gives rise to the Bodhi-mind and upholds this sutra — even just four lines of it, reading, reciting, and explaining it to others — their merit would surpass that of the former.

How should one explain it to others?
Do not attach to appearances, remain unmoved.

Why is this so?

> All conditioned phenomena
> Are like a dream, an illusion, a bubble, a shadow,
> Like dew or a flash of lightning;
> Thus shall we perceive them."

After the Buddha finished speaking this sutra, the elder Subhuti, together with the monks, nuns, male and female lay followers, and all beings in the world, the devas, humans, and asuras, heard what the Buddha said, rejoiced greatly, and faithfully accepted and practiced it.

Translated by Julie Zhu

Appendix:

The Heart of the Perfection of Wisdom Sutra

TRANSLATED TO CHINESE BY THE TANG DYNASTY TRIPIṬAKA MASTER XUANZANG

TRANSLATED TO ENGLISH BY JULIE ZHU

When the Bodhisattva Avalokitesvarawas practicing the profound Prajnaparamita, he perceived that the five aggregates (FORM, SENSATION, PERCEPTION, MENTAL FORMATIONS, CONSCIOUSNESS) are all empty, and thus he overcame all suffering and distress.

Sariputra, form does not differ from emptiness, and emptiness does not differ from form. Form itself is emptiness, and emptiness itself is form. The same is true of sensation, perception, mental formations, and consciousness.

Sariputra, all dharmas are marked with emptiness; they do not arise or cease, are not defiled or pure, do not increase or decrease.

Therefore, in emptiness there is no form, no sensation, perception, mental formations, or consciousness; no eye, ear, nose, tongue, body, or mind; no form, sound, smell, taste, touch, or dharma; no realm of the eye, … up to no realm of consciousness.

There is no ignorance and no extinction of ignorance; … up to no aging and death, and no extinction of aging and death; no suffering, cause of suffering, cessation, or path; no wisdom and no attainment.

Because there is nothing to be attained, the Bodhisattva relies on Prajnaparamita and thus has no obstruction in the mind. Because there is no obstruction, there is no fear; far beyond deluded thoughts and dreams, he reaches ultimate Nirvana.

All Buddhas of the past, present, and future rely on Prajnaparamita and attain ANUTTARA SAMYAKSAMBODHI.

Therefore, know that Prajnaparamita is the greatest mantra, the brightest mantra, the supreme mantra, the unequaled mantra; it can remove all suffering, and it is true and not false.

Therefore, the mantra of Prajnaparamita is spoken, which is:

"Gate gate paragate parasamgate bodhi svaha."

www.ingramcontent.com/pod-product-compliance
Lightning Source LLC
Chambersburg PA
CBHW052124070526
44586CB00016B/2067